The Things You Have to Do Before I Buy You a Phone

Adam Ferguson

GREENLEAF
BOOK GROUP PRESS

Published by Greenleaf Book Group Press
Austin, Texas
www.gbgpress.com

Distributed by Greenleaf Book Group

For ordering information or special discounts for bulk purchases, please contact Greenleaf Book Group at PO Box 91869, Austin, TX 78709, 512.891.6100.

Design and composition by Greenleaf Book Group
Cover design by Greenleaf Book Group and Brian Phillips
Illustrations by David Ferguson

Publisher's Cataloging-in-Publication data is available.

Print ISBN: 979-8-88645-364-5

eBook ISBN: 979-8-88645-365-2

To offset the number of trees consumed in the printing of our books, Greenleaf donates a portion of the proceeds from each printing to the Arbor Day Foundation. Greenleaf Book Group has replaced over 50,000 trees since 2007.

Printed in the United States of America on acid-free paper

25 26 27 28 29 30 31   10 9 8 7 6 5 4 3 2 1

First Edition

For my kids.
And for your kids.

To the Grown-Ups

Want to hear a crazy stat? In the 1960s, almost half of American adults regularly smoked cigarettes. And actual doctors in actual advertisements assured us certain brands were "less irritating!" and "more throat friendly!" And then, decades later, after all that lung cancer, we got to look back and wonder what on earth we were thinking.

Twenty years from now, none of us wants to ask that same question about kids and smartphones. Yes, we all recognize that the phone's an awesome tool—world-changing awesome—but we're also reckoning with its side effects. How it's sapping our attention. Isolating us from one another, fracturing our human bonds. Disconnecting us from nature. Messing with our mental health. I think we can recognize the light havoc that phones, despite all their conveniences, have sprinkled across society. And even though we don't totally understand why or how to fix it . . . we hand them to sixth graders.

This book doesn't suggest we deny our kids digital connectivity altogether. But it is recommending an *interruption*. It's a guidebook, with a handful of lessons we seem to be skipping, that aims to interrupt what feels like a reckless handoff of tech to kids. And it's an attempt to resurrect core childhood. Because what we're doing today isn't working.

What will your kids get from running this gauntlet? A little bit of knowledge about life's basics, practical knowledge about how things work, and maybe some theoretical knowledge about why they matter. They'll confront the unfamiliar, the somewhat risky, and probably a handful of fears. They'll learn to combat boredom with curiosity and creativity. But most importantly, they'll gain self-reliance. The courage to start adventuring into the world on their own, safely, in small steps. Because we all want strong, independent kids.

These tasks may not be universally applicable to your kid's life—for instance, you might live in a city where riding a bike is unsafe, or they may not have siblings to babysit—so feel free to interpret the lessons within the tasks and adapt them for your own household. Also, some of these skills might be new to you, even as parents—you may not have experience growing plants or playing chess. That's OK; some of them are meant to be learned alongside your kid. In fact, it's kind of better that way. My hope is this book not only shapes your kids in fifty different ways but that it gives you fifty chances to bond with them too.

However you approach the list, there are a lot of important life lessons captured within. And as your kids grudgingly work through them, they'll hopefully gain some valuable skills along the way, until arriving at that beautiful, messy, coming-of-age rite of passage, that preteen holy grail: the phone.

Good luck. Let's get to convincing.

—Adam

To the Kids

Hey, kiddo. You're about to hit adolescence, and I'm here to hand off a bit of hard-earned grown-up wisdom: Punching your thumbs against a screen isn't real life. Not even close.

"Look around, old timer," you'll say. "Yeah, it is." And I fully acknowledge that you're growing up at a time in human history where we're all tangled up with technology. One day, people will expect you to know how to work with it, so you'll want to keep your head in that game. But I'm not really worried about you there. You're what they call a "digital native."

What I do worry about is the possibility of too much tech disconnecting you from your basic humanness. Your place in the natural world. Your sense of compassion for others, which is so strong in you right now. That's some of what I've seen these phones strip away. And not to mention the basic life skills you're gonna need as you get older. Why should you learn how to cook a meal when food delivery is a couple taps away? Or learn to write when AI can just make the words up for you? Because learning how to rely on yourself—in any and all situations—is the best gift that we grown-ups can give you. You don't want the phone becoming a crutch you use for so long that you forget how to walk on your own.

So, here are fifty things you have to do before we buy you a phone. Some of them you'll be able to do solo; some, you'll need our help with. My hope is that, as you knock them out, you'll gain a better understanding of yourself, your work ethic, your creative instincts, how to survive in this world should the power go out, and how to care for others. You know, the basics.

I know the phone looks like everything these days because everybody's playing with it all the time. And I know the tech is captivating—it's a nonstop entertainment machine—but I'm here to tell you: *There's so much more to life.*

This is gonna be fun. Let's get going.

—Adam and the rest of the grown-ups

All the Things

1. Do the laundry.
2. Play a game of chess.
3. Get paid for a skill.
4. Sit in a room. For fifteen minutes. Without doing anything.
5. Write a thank-you note. Make it count.
6. Do the grocery shopping.
7. Cook a full dinner. Serve it to the family. Clean up.
8. Babysit for a night.
9. Make me a playlist.
10. Bike to a friend's house and back, at least a half mile away.
11. Spend some time with old folks.
12. Play me one-on-one in basketball. A full game, to twenty-one.
13. Go for a long walk in the wild.
14. Grow a vegetable from seed.
15. Catch a fish.
16. Approach someone you don't know well.
17. Come to work with me for a day.
18. Play me a song on an instrument.
19. Record your thoughts in a journal for a month.
20. Write down five questions you've always wanted answers to. I'll do my best to answer them.
21. Attend a religious service or two.
22. Write down your top ten beliefs.
23. Run a 5k.

24. Go on a weekend road trip with me.
25. Clean the bathroom.
26. Spend a night in the woods camping.
27. Learn to throw a punch.
28. Make your own lunch for school.
29. Buy or make a gift for someone.
30. Volunteer your time for the community.
31. Write me a letter.
32. Explain to me how the phone actually works.
33. Get first aid certified.
34. Walk your brother or sister to school.
35. Care for an animal.
36. Eat vegetarian for one week.
37. Tell me what's going on in the world.
38. Tour the local police or fire station.
39. Break a (minor) law.
40. Build something out of wood with me.
41. Read a book.
42. Pick a location at least two miles from home.
Navigate us there without GPS.
43. Memorize a poem.
44. Visit a cemetery.
45. Swim one hundred meters.
46. Build a fire.
47. Let me take you and your friends somewhere to hang out.
48. Save enough money to buy the phone yourself.
49. Manage that money in a bank.
50. Turn fourteen.

1 Do the Laundry.

I bet clean clothes seem pretty magical right now—they just "arrive" in your room. But recognize that that's your parents doing you a solid, week after week after week. And since it's a skill everyone needs to know eventually, I'm going to teach you how to do the laundry.

The reason you wash your clothes is basically bugs. If you don't wash them, your T-shirts and shorts and underwear will collect tiny vermin, like fleas and bedbugs, and nobody wants bugs in their underwear. You also wash your clothes because looking somewhat put together communicates safety to other people. It's a weird animal truth. "That person is so fresh, so clean. They must not be a threat."

All that said, you can get a couple wears out of a sweatshirt. Unless there's a three-fingered streak of barbecue sauce down the front or a noticeably off smell, you're probably fine. I'd actually advise you to be thoughtful about what you toss into the hamper because the more clothes you dump in, the more there is to wash, the more water gets used, etc.

The washer and dryer aren't tough to operate; I'll show you how. A full week of this will get the process locked into your head. Also, remember: The trick isn't complete unless you stick the landing. In other words, this task isn't done until the laundry is folded and put away in drawers.

2
Play a Game of Chess.

When you think *game*, I bet your brain starts mashing a handheld controller. But games are as old as human history, and *Fortnite*'s only been around since 2017. For this task, you're going to square up against me in a game that's fifteen hundred years old.

Chess is the game of kings and queens and knights and pawns. Two people face each other over a checkered board, engaging in epic battles. One at a time, you ruthlessly kill off the other player's pieces using nothing more than the power of your brain.

But more important than game play, chess teaches you to see things from the other person's perspective. Because when you can see all their pieces, you can track their decisions, and if you can track their decisions, you'll be able to learn how they think to anticipate their next move. Which can, in turn, help you figure out your own strategies.

And *that* is the life lesson that chess unlocks. One of the tricks to "getting good at people" is being able to see things from other perspectives. You'll need this skill not only to conquer opponents but to solve problems when you're working in teams and to help the people you love get through their stuff. It's kind of invaluable.

Chess isn't easy; it's not checkers. It might take us a few practice rounds to get it right. But there was this kid, Bobby Fischer, who was beating grown-up experts in chess when he was ten years old, so no excuses. Kids can do big, hard things.

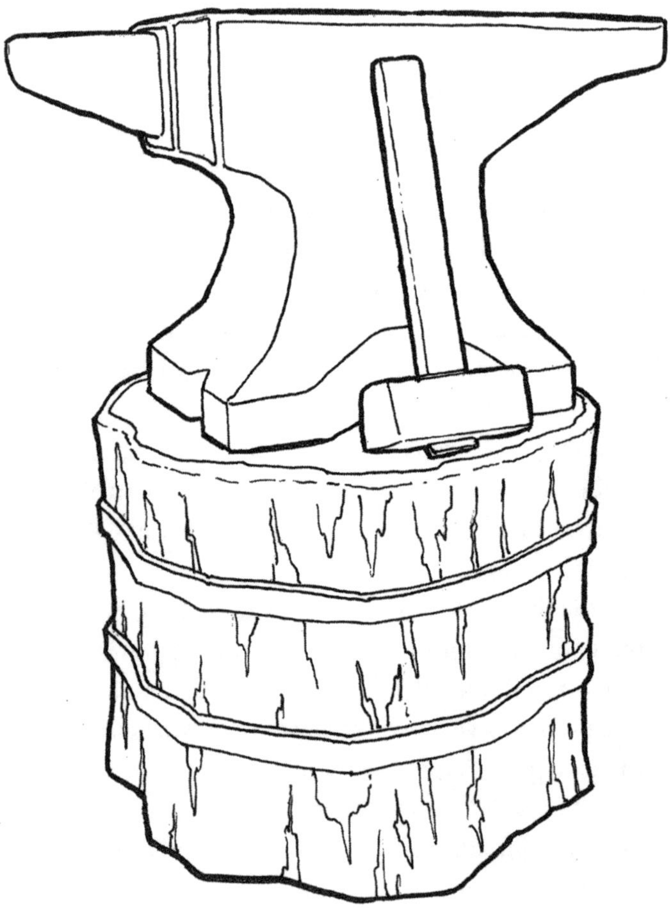

3 Get Paid for a Skill.

Adults work for a living. You know that, right? Every day, they go out into the world and perform services. And because others find value in those services, people earn money.

Now, money is just an imaginary concept made up by humans to represent value, but it's a concept that keeps civilization flowing. It's how we're all able to get stuff. Right now, I pay for a lot of your stuff, but as you grow up, money is going to occupy more of your attention. And it's a bit of a game you'll have to learn.

There was once this kid who tried to get people on her block to pay her for ghostbusting. She put flyers on their doors advertising services ("Ectoplasm removal!"), but the only call she got was from some older kids pranking her. Her ghostbuster career didn't work out because it wasn't a skill people valued.

But eventually, she got paid for babysitting. She entertained seven-year-olds with games, made them dinner, kept them safe, got them to bed. After that, she worked in grocery stores, restaurants, coffee shops. She formed a rock band with her friends, and they got paid for their shows. She found valuable skills inside herself.

The point is, an important part of life is proving to yourself that you can find a way to be of value to others—enough that it puts money in your pocket. We're beyond lemonade stands here. I'm looking for something that demonstrates your unique skills. And you know what? You have lots of skills. Those muscles can rake leaves or shovel driveways. That brain can design T-shirts or bracelets. I'm happy to think on it with you.

4 Sit in a Room. For Fifteen Minutes. Without Doing Anything.

Just sit in one spot and chill. You can do that for fifteen minutes, right? Totally easy? Maybe not. Here are the rules.

You have to sit up. You can't sleep; you can't even lie down. And you have to sit still—no getting up and moving around. You can't read or look through books. You definitely can't look at screens. You just have to sit. It's OK to close your eyes if you feel like it, but for sure close your mouth. Shhhh . . . just sit.

I know you think this is a simple one, but it's hard to be bored, especially in this age of all-day, everyday beep-boop. There's always something digital grabbing at our attention. We so rarely just chill with ourselves.

I'll tell you a secret, though—some of your best ideas will bloom during your quietest moments, like when you're taking a walk or standing in the shower or when you're riding on a train, staring out the window. When the distractions split, when our brains stop consuming information, that's when the dots connect and the sparks fly. Those quiet moments are also the best times to get to know yourself—and that's by far the most important relationship you'll create in this life.

Let me know when you're going to do this task, and I'll time you. When you're done, I'd love to hear what thoughts went through your brain.

THANK YOU!

Write a Thank-You Note. 5 Make It Count.

Every once in a while, someone will do something nice for you. Sure, they'll give you a present on your birthday, but that's expected. It's the *unexpected* nice that sticks with you—like breaking a candy bar at lunch and giving you half, or inviting you to a movie, or even just stopping to ask if you're doing all right on a day when you're not.

In those moments, you might feel this wave of emotion rush through you. *That was so nice.* And you might not know what to do with that wave. But here's a great way to ride it: Write them a thank-you note.

A real thank-you note, not a text message. Texts are easy; we dash them off in seconds. I'm talking about thoughtful pen to paper plus delivery. Making the full thank-you note effort communicates a deeper gratitude because of the extra time it takes. And even though it's really not that much time or effort, if you do a good job, they'll remember it down the road and always think a little better of you.

That's why the "make it count" part of this challenge matters. Don't just dash off a "Thanks for the present, bro. Love, me." Sit with your thoughts for a second. Try to figure out why their small act of kindness mattered to you. Challenge yourself to make them feel that same wave of emotion. You'll know you pulled it off when whoever you thanked calls me and says, "That was so nice."

6

Do the Grocery Shopping.

I will write the shopping list. I will drive you to the grocery store. I will give you a credit and/or debit card. But then you're on your own, kid. It's up to you to walk the aisles and fill the cart. It's up to you to pioneer an expedition through a strange land. I will wait in the parking lot for you to come outside with a week's worth of groceries.

(Are you 😳 yet?)

You'll have to navigate the store all by yourself, reading the signs and labels to locate things. You may have to reach up tall shelves or ask someone for help along the way. That's all right. There are lots of good people in a grocery store, ready to help. Just keep pushing that cart; keep crossing the next thing off your list. You can do this. Anyway, it ends up being kind of fun.

And if you come out with an unsanctioned box of donuts, carton of ice cream, or pack of gum . . . I'll look the other way.

7

Cook a Full Dinner. Serve It to the Family. Clean Up.

The number one question I'm asked in this house: "Hey, what's for dinner?" And every day, like an absolute boss, I answer that question. Now, it's your turn.

Cooking is fun. Heck, it's a chance to work with knives and fire. It's also a chance to be creative. You get to throw ingredients together and show other people what tastes you're into. And most importantly, it's a chance to show your family how much you love them, because cooking is hard work, man. As your parent, I get to cook dinner for the full family a lot of nights, and despite the hard work, it makes me feel good seeing good food go into your bodies (even when it's something new and WEIRD, and you'll only take one bite).

So figure out your menu. Spaghetti and meatballs? Roast chicken? Taco Tuesday? I'll help buy the ingredients and get you set up, but you'll be the one in charge of the stove and all the other hardware. Don't worry, I'll be there to make sure you don't hurt yourself. And then, after everyone is happy and full and complimenting your incredible kitchen skills, only then will you get the thankless job of cleaning up the mess.

But hey, here's the good news: After all that work, you'll appreciate what goes into making dinner, and that means from then on, I'll get an extra big hug on your way to bed.

NEED
A
RELIABLE
BABY
SITTER?
★GREAT REFERENCES★
LIAM 000·000·0000
LIAM 000·000·0000
LIAM 000·000·0000
LIAM 000·000·0000
LIAM 000·000·0000
LIAM 000·000·0000

8 Babysit for a Night.

This is a big one, but the test is simple: How do you handle the responsibility of 100 percent trust? Dinner, lights, locks, bedtimes. Normally, your parents handle all that, but tonight, we're relying on you.

For these few hours, you'll be on your own, calling all the shots. Kind of scary, right? What if the smoke alarm goes off? What if someone throws up? You're the one who will have to figure it out.

Here's a trick for your brain, though, and it's a trick you can use forever: On the other side of Scary is Cool. *Oh no, I have to run the show?! Hey, wait . . . I* get *to run the show!* The whole night will be yours, so what'll you make of it? Forts? Epic hide-and-seek? Water pistol throwdown? It's yours to decide, kiddo. Just keep everyone safe while you're having fun. That's the number one rule.

Once you get everyone to brush their teeth and go to bed, you'll have that sweet relief of the house to yourself. You can watch a movie, play a video game. Just keep your ears open—someone may want a glass of water or have a bad dream. They may need your help. And that's your job tonight. That's why you're there.

Bonus points if the house looks better than when you started once I get home.

[If you don't have any siblings, a friend's or neighbor's children will do.]*

A
Hannah's Mix Tape

9 Make Me a Playlist.

Long, long ago, people made mixtapes for one another. Each tape was carefully assembled to create a vibe. What should the first song be? A banger? And then what should come next, maybe some unexpected sweetness? The order of the songs was important because there was no "shuffle" back then—you built the order, and your order told a story.

What kinds of stories? Well, that depended on the coded message you were trying to send. For example, if it was a mixtape for someone you liked, you chose songs to make them feel all romantic. But a tape for a road trip with friends? Totally different vibe.

Hearing your playlist will tell me a lot about what you're into right now, but it might also tell me how you want me to feel about you, if that makes any sense. The music we play sends messages. I guess I just want to get into your head and heart, and your tunes are a great doorway.

So make me a playlist on Spotify or YouTube or Apple Music. Fifteen to twenty songs should do it. I want to know what bops you're into. Tell me a story.

10

Bike to a Friend's House and Back, at Least a Half Mile Away.

You learned to ride a bike in first grade on the street outside our house, and I remember watching you pedal away. You made it all the way down the street, and then just . . . kept going. Right around the corner, until I couldn't see you anymore. It was an immediate panic. Oh no. There goes my kid. Into the world. Without my protection.

All parents face this moment: learning to let their kids go. Allowing them to grow up. And reminding themselves that the world isn't something to be feared—that it's a wild and beautiful place, waiting for you to explore it. I want that courage for you, that fearlessness. I want you in the world, staring down the unknown. And that starts with me letting you go out on your own.

So pick a friend who lives at least a half mile away from us, and ride your bike to their house. Try to stay on the sidewalk. If you have to ride on the streets, it's all right—just stay on the right side, and watch for cars. And have their parents call me when you get there. And wear a helmet, would you?

Man, I worry too much. You're strong, brave, and capable. You'll figure it out.

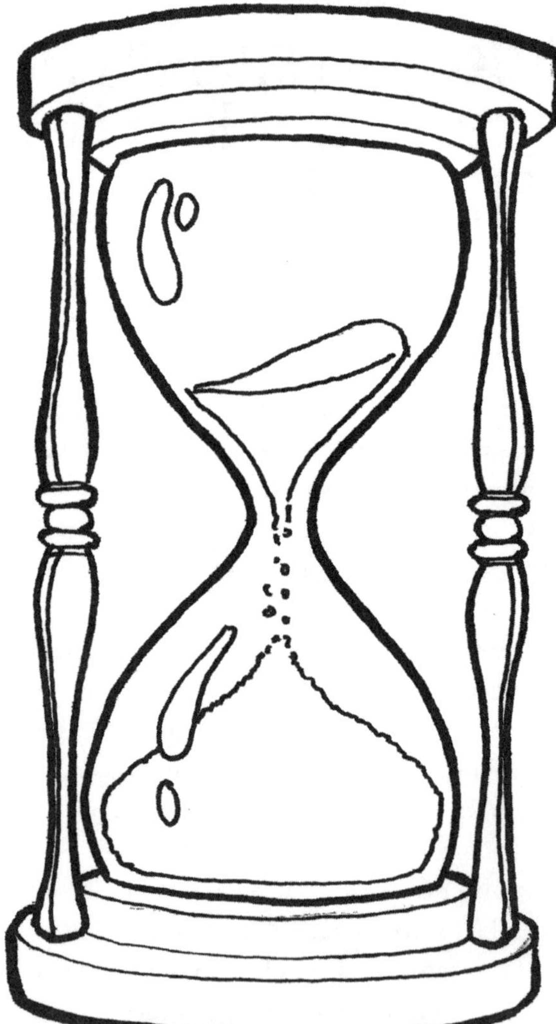

11 Spend Some Time with Old Folks.

Am I the old person you're thinking of right now? Oh boy, I am not old. I'm kind of in the middle of my life, hopefully. You should be thinking about people in their seventies or eighties. Those are the "old folks" I'm talking about.

Old people used to be really valuable to younger people because they could pass on crazy amounts of knowledge. But since your generation has the internet at its fingertips—which is basically access to all the world's knowledge—it begs the question: Why do I want you to do this task? What's to be gained from time spent with an old person?

And the answer is because they deserve it. In this era you're living through, which is so exciting with all the "new" and "what's next?" energy, older people have kind of been forgotten. We've accidentally shuffled them off to the sidelines. And as a result, some of them are lonely. But they spent their lives raising kids just like you, putting the hard work in, and you know what? They deserve our attention from time to time.

For this task, it's cool if you want to pick a grandparent and have dinner with them. But it'll be important for it to be just you and them—just the two of you, no big family noise and distractions. Or if that doesn't work, we can visit a senior center or retirement complex. I'm sure they have programs where they need volunteers.

I think you'll get a lot out of it. At the very least, I know you'll make them very happy. And sometimes, that's enough.

12

Play Me One-on-One in Basketball. A Full Game, to Twenty-One.

Let's gooo!

You pick the court, name the time, and the throwdown will begin.

I will not go easy on you.

I will bring the heat.

And my hope is this will be the first game of many. You may not win the first go-round, but I guarantee you'll beat me eventually. Because every day, I am getting older and creakier, and you are getting bigger and stronger, and that is just the natural order of things.

Honestly, I can't wait for the day you beat me—on your own merit, with your own strength and skills, maybe with a crossover and reverse layup. I want nothing more than for my children to surpass the summits I've climbed.

[Other one-on-one sports—Ping-Pong, bowling, a game of pool—can also apply.]*

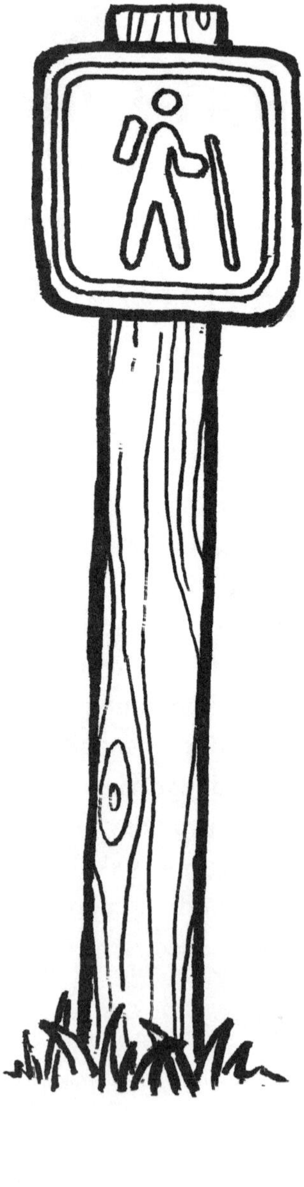

13 Go for a Long Walk in the Wild.

If you ever need to clear out your mental pipes, drop everything and take a walk. There's nothing like a blast of the outdoors for rebooting your head. Move your legs, drink up the fresh air, and your worries will be left in your wake. And if you ever need to *deep* clean your mental pipes—like, shine the chrome to a polish—take a walk in the woods.

For this task, I can find us a trail, with markers. Or a canyon, or a gulch—maybe one that follows a river. Heck, I can probably find us a mountain, if you're up for it. It might require a drive, but there are lots of mountains we can get up and down in a day. We'll just need some decent shoes.

Climbing a big hill—or taking a long hike with a scenic overlook—will give you a lot: It'll teach you to find rhythm inside monotony and unlock your grit. It'll remind you that the natural world is both majestic and indifferent to your existence. When you get up high enough, to a place where you can see the earth spread beneath your feet, you gain a sense of yourself—how you fit within the bigger picture, how small your worries are.

I'll do this one with you. We'll find a good long day hike nearby and humble ourselves before nature. I think I'm most looking forward to the conversation. When you're hiking, all you can do (besides walk) is talk to each other, and the conversations can detour to some weird, wonderful territory.

14 Grow a Vegetable from Seed.

Here's one you can't race to check off the list. It's going to tap your patience. And all kids have oceans of patience, right? And all kids love vegetables, right?

The cool part about growing a vegetable from seed is the godlike powers. You will literally be creating food from the ground. Most of us take an easy trip to the store for vegetables and fruits, forgetting that we're reliant on the hard work of farmers. But not you, not this time. You will draw life from the earth, all by yourself.

There are two ways we could go about this. The first is to buy a bunch of seeds at the hardware store—cucumbers, carrots, arugula—and plant them in the backyard. We'll build some kind of plot and surround it with chicken wire so that bunnies and squirrels can't crash in and eat everything. And eventually, we'll have a backyard crop. It's pretty satisfying to eat food you've grown yourself.

The second, simpler approach is to grow your plant(s) in a pot on the windowsill. It's still a big responsibility. You'll have to give it a little bit of your attention every day. Plants need water and sunlight, and they'll be relying on you to deliver them. Weirdly, they also like it when you talk to them. Make sure to do some research on how to care for whatever seeds we buy so that the water–sunlight mix is just right.

One final, important note: You've only completed this task when we can take a big bite of your end result. It'll be delicious. Vegetables, ho!

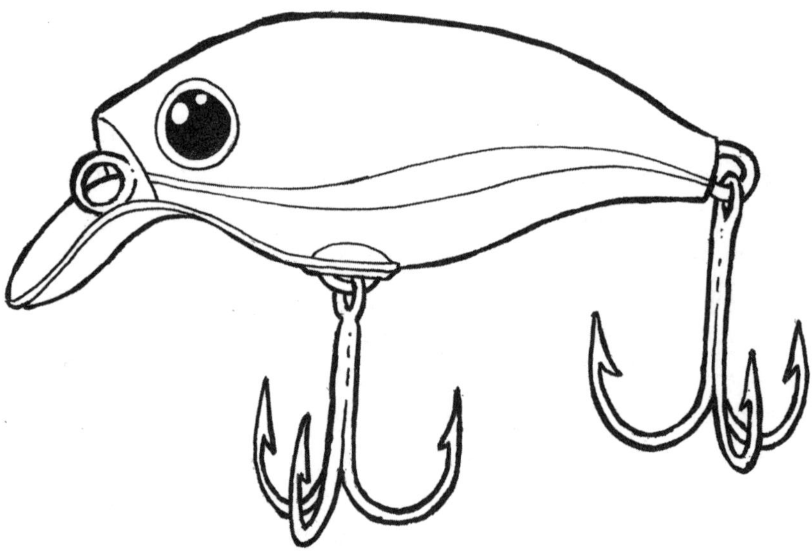

15 Catch a Fish.

This world you live in is bustling with life. Go look outside. There's people, dogs, cats, birds and bugs, trees and weeds and bushes. Everything's alive.

And one of the uncomfortable truths about life is that survival comes at a cost. When you eat bacon, you're eating part of a pig. At one point, that pig was alive, rolling around in the grass and mud with its brothers and sisters, but then farmers took its life so that ours could continue. It's a gnarly little truth but an important one to face. Bacon might feel like a short, neatly packaged trip to the grocery store, but that's only because our systems are protecting you from the hard part—raising the animal and killing it so that it can become food.

This challenge is about facing that truth: that humans are predators, and our prey are chickens, pigs, cows, goats, and so on. At your age, the closest I can get you to this truth without grossing you out too much is by fishing.

Fishing's actually kind of nice. You find a patch of water, sit in the sun, and wait for the line to tug. That's the fish nibbling your bait. Then, you fight with it—you try to pull the fish up out of the water while it tries to break free. If you win the fight and the fish is big enough to eat, we'll clean it, cook it, eat it, and most importantly, we'll give it thanks for the life that it's given to us.

16 Approach Someone You Don't Know Well.

One thing you'll learn about phones: people use them to hide. You've probably seen it at school—when kids feel alone, even for a minute, they pull out their devices and . . . separate. They dip from the real world. And they do it because thumbs on screens are a lot easier to deal with than people, who are unpredictable and complicated and don't always act the way you want them to.

This might be the most important lesson in this book: Feeling uncomfortable around other people is normal. Everyone—and I do mean everyone—is a little anxious about how they're being perceived by others. It's like an animal instinct. My advice to you: Fight through that discomfort, and do your best to connect with people anyway. Remind yourself how cool you are, put a brave face on, and put yourself out there, fearlessly. Because those connections you'll make—with friends or even (gulp) boyfriends/girlfriends—are the glue that'll hold everything together when the rest of your life quakes.

For this task, you've got to work up the courage to talk to a kid your age who you're kind of interested in but don't know that well. Face-to-face. Eye contact. Oooh, it's gonna be uncomfortable. You're gonna have to dig deep to get past that discomfort. And it may go perfectly, or it may sputter out, but that's the fire of life. To access the best parts, you need to take some risks.

Either way, go easy on yourself. You're cooler than a lot of people I know. If you need an opening line, try "Hey, want to do something after school?"

17 Come to Work with Me for a Day.

Five days of every week, most of us grown-ups rouse ourselves from bed, grab a shower and a cup of coffee, and head to work. To you, that might sound like a grind—and some days, it is—but lots of people actually like what they do. We find meaning in our work.

Right now, your only job is school. (And you've still got ten to fifteen years in front of you!) But someday, you'll very likely have a paying job. And my sincere hope is that you never have to settle for work that doesn't get your mind and heart pumping. I hope you hop out of bed with just an edge of motivation, loving the work part of your life a little bit.

Come with me for a day to the world of grown-ups, and watch us work together. You'll see us talk through problems, figure out ways to solve them, and make decisions. You'll watch us make things. What are these grown-ups trying to do? What world are they trying to create? Your job will be to sit quietly, watch, and listen. I'll be interested to hear your thoughts at the end of the day.

It might be a little boring for you, but hey, at least we'll get to spend some time together. And in the days to come, if your friends ask you what I do, you'll be able to paint a picture for them.

18

Play Me a Song on an Instrument.

You say you want to grab a kazoo and hum "Happy Birthday" at me? OK, that counts. That's an instrument; that's a song. But just listen for a minute to what this task is trying to accomplish for you.

Music taps something deep in our soul's molten core, makes us *feel* in a way that I'm honestly not sure any other art form can. Movies, painting, writing—they're all amazing and important—but only music gets us dancing and singing.

If I could give you one gift in this life, it would be the ability to play an instrument. Let's not kid ourselves, it's work: The piano has eighty-eight keys; the guitar's strings will crunch your fingers at first. But I promise you, get past the hard parts, and it's full-on magic. And then, you'll have a place you can go your whole life, a place to retreat from the chaos, just you and your fingers and your breath and your mind, making songs to fill the air.

To do this task right, pick out your favorite song, and try to figure it out on whichever musical instrument you're into. Use your ears, use your fingers, and just play around. If we don't own your instrument of choice, let's check your school, or maybe we know someone who can lend us one. Also, YouTube is a great resource for learning notes and chords; you can find lessons for almost any song.

All said and done, if you do go the kazoo/"Happy Birthday" route, then kid, your rendition better blow my hair back.

JOURNAL

19 Record Your Thoughts in a Journal for a Month.

Life moves pretty fast, doesn't it? Most of our days are occupied with things to do, and when the things to do are done, we amuse ourselves with distractions. Work and play. If it's well balanced, that's a pretty fun existence.

But as the scenery flies by, a lot of us forget to slow the ride and make sense of where we are. That's true of kids and adults. We get swept up in the flow. My guess is that inside your brain, it's mile-a-minute chatter. There are good things happening up there—you're making sense of the world—and it gets really interesting when you grab a pen and a notebook and slow things down for a few minutes.

Write about anything—things that happened to you during the day, things you saw, ideas you had, feelings you felt, or maybe just a fun story you want to make up. Some days, the words will come slowly, and you'll have to think hard to piece it together, and some days, they'll come so fast, you'll scorch the page. The important thing is making time for a sit-down conversation with yourself.

I'm asking you to do this every day for a month, but secretly, I'm hoping it becomes a lifelong practice—a way for you to make sense of the world.

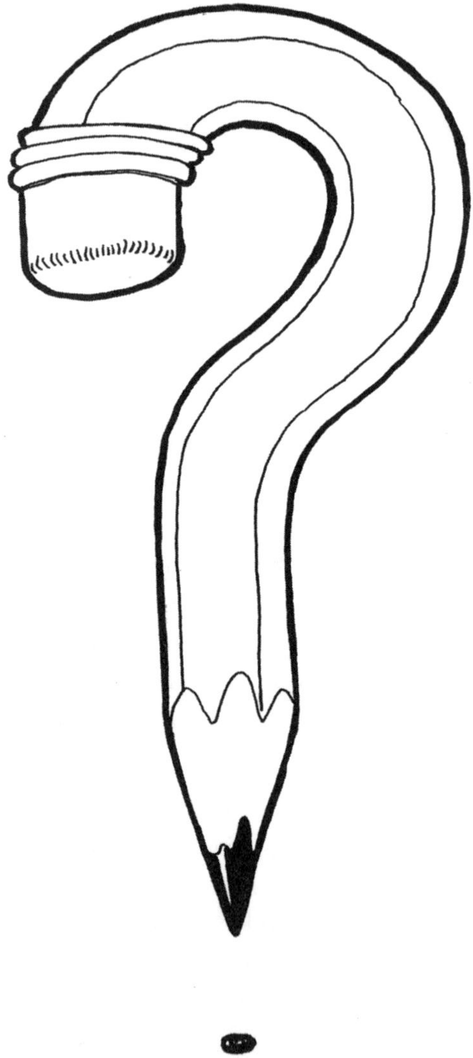

20 Write Down Five Questions You've Always Wanted Answers to. I'll Do My Best to Answer Them.

In your decade or so on this earth, what big stuff have you been wondering about? Not the questions that can be easily answered by the internet—the big stuff.

Maybe you're wondering about the meaning of life, or the meaning of your life, or the meaning of my life. Maybe you're wondering why kids are mean sometimes, or why wars happen, or whether birds are real, or whether God is real. This is your chance. Ask me some big ones. Swing for the fences.

But just do me a favor: Take a minute and give this some real thought. Come up with five questions that you feel, if answered, might change the way you look at life. If you can do that, then I can make a promise back to you: I will dig deep and put a lot of thought into the answers. (And by the way, asking me the big questions is an open invitation; I'm always available to knock ideas around with you.)

Why? Because I love you, kiddo. And if something's important to you, then it's important to me too.

21

Attend a Religious Service or Two.

The idea of God is super important to a lot of people. With zero proof, they believe in an all-knowing power that created us, loves us, and wants the best for us. It's kind of a nice idea, that we're being watched over. It certainly takes bravery to believe in something so fundamental to your existence but that you can't ever prove.

I think you know this already: People don't just believe in a single god. There are different religions, different gods, all with different rules and ideas. In our community, there are Christians, Jews, Muslims, Hindus, and probably some others. Which of them is right? Well, it's impossible to know. What's cool, though, is that all these different people are wrestling to live their lives meaningfully. They're talking with each other about the big stuff: existence and the human condition and how to do the right thing.

Each of these groups meet up regularly in their churches or temples to talk about their gods. So for this task, we're going to visit one service at each place and find out how they're different and how they're the same. I'll accompany you. They'll be quick, and we'll learn a lot. We'll see God through the eyes of others. It should give us a lot to talk about.

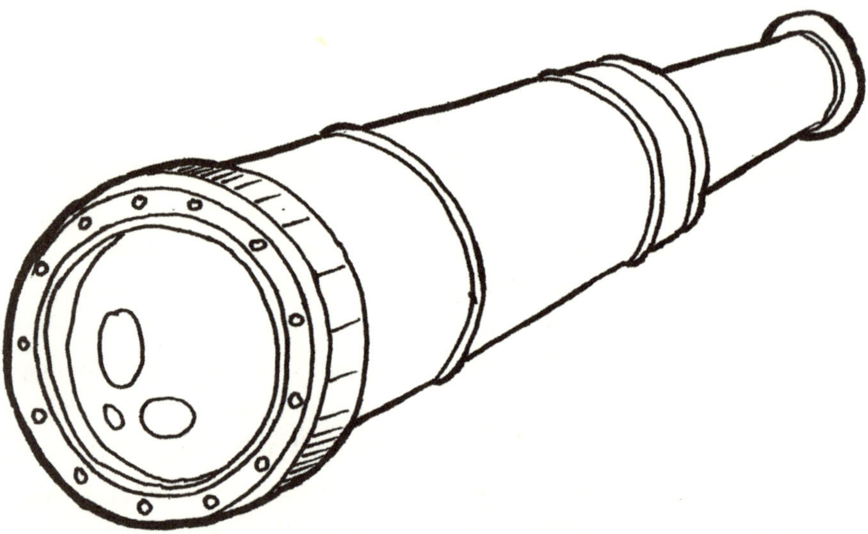

22 Write Down Your Top Ten Beliefs.

Now that we've covered the bravery of believing in something, I want to know what *you've* come to believe so far. What have you learned in your short time on this planet?

Take a couple minutes to write down ten things you believe to be true. It could be major-league stuff, like "I believe people are inherently good," or simple stuff, like "I believe hamburgers are the president of food." These are your beliefs, though, and they'll reveal a little about your soul. Take them seriously. Make a good-faith effort to get them right.

1. I believe ______________________________.
2. I believe ______________________________.
3. I believe ______________________________.
4. I believe ______________________________.
5. I believe ______________________________.
6. I believe ______________________________.
7. I believe ______________________________.
8. I believe ______________________________.
9. I believe ______________________________.
10. I believe ______________________________.

23 Run a 5k.

5k = 5 kilometers.

5 kilometers = 3.1 miles.

3.1 miles = roughly 25–30 minutes of continuous running, for the untrained runner.

Let's just get this out of the way: The first mile's gonna suck. You're going to want to bail out. But that's your brain talking, not your body. You're young; you're built for this kind of thing. If you can fight past that first mile, your body will find this beautiful rhythm, your brain will start to glow, and the rest of the run will come easy. I promise: It's "the runner's high," and it's real.

Locating enough inner patience to get through that first mile is a big part of this task. It's called endurance, kiddo, and you're gonna need to know how to tap into it throughout your life, how to push back on your brain when it tells you, "This is too hard."

It's also important in this life to regularly get your heart pumping, your blood moving. Your body is a machine that needs to be worked if you want it to stay tuned.

To get started, I would suggest a couple practice runs—maybe a half mile to begin with, working your way up to 3.1. And then, who knows, maybe you'll keep going.

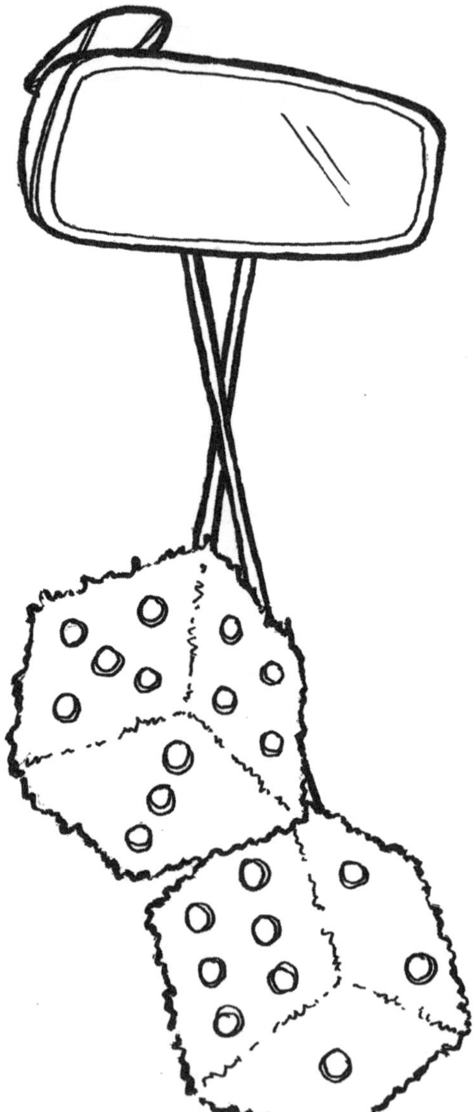

24 Go on a Weekend Road Trip with Me.

I bet within a couple hours' drive, there's an interesting spot for us to visit. A state park. A cool city with cool things to do. A family member or a long-lost friend.

We might pass an out-of-the-blue sign for something like a corn palace, and we might detour for a minute. (We would definitely detour for that.) Or we might get hungry and pull over at the truck stop with the full parking lot and, whoa, the best french fries. We might get lost, but we'll get found again. The important thing is the trip itself. Giving ourselves the room to meander, to lose timelines, to just hang with each other and watch the scenery go by.

An open highway. A tank full of gas or a battery full of juice. Windows down, sun on your face, your hand sliding over the wind. There's no greater sense of freedom.

We'll pick a spot. We'll put your playlist on (see task nine). I think it'd be kind of cool if it was just you and me, but your call.

25 Clean the Bathroom.

This sounds easy. It is not easy.

Cleaning the bathroom properly—spraying, wiping down, getting on your knees to scrub behind the toilet—takes a decent amount of effort. I will arm you with soap, a sponge, a brush, a couple dry rags, and probably some other stuff. You will be loaded up like a dirt warrior, ready to hunt down every offending speck.

I could've chosen the kitchen, the TV room, or your bedroom. Why the bathroom? Because it's gross. You'll come across long stray hairs, blobs of white-ish lotion, unexplainable wet spots. You might even find a bug that needs liberation—they love the moisture. I chose the bathroom because getting your hands dirty occasionally is good for you. Touching the Gross teaches you that you can survive touching the Gross. And besides, you're a handwash away from back-to-normal. No biggie.

I just want to put you through these paces one time. Because as your parent, I've done it for years, and now you can do it with me. One time.

That's right, I said "with me." I'll give you jobs and show you how it's done. You're not Little Orphan Annie; we're in this together.

And then at the end . . . clean bathroom. Which is nice.

(Bonus points if you straighten up the medicine cabinet.)

26 Spend a Night in the Woods Camping.

It's hard to be free of noise anymore. Stop and listen for a second. Is there an airplane overhead? Did the furnace just kick in? Is some device chiming at you? And don't forget the visual noise of TV screens, street traffic, hustle, bustle, and so on. The world runs on power. And power creates noise.

But head into the woods and you'll reconnect with something inside yourself—something that's much older, almost ancient. Set up your tent. Light a fire when it gets dark. Notice the quiet. In the darkness, you'll hear a soft wind rustle the leaves. You'll hear animals moving through the brush. It can be uncomfortable, that kind of quiet, until you remember: Oh yeah, you're an animal too. You're supposed to be here. You're part of this story.

Let's see if we can spend at least one night in the woods. Settling into the quiet of nature builds a new strength inside you. I'll come along and show you the ropes.

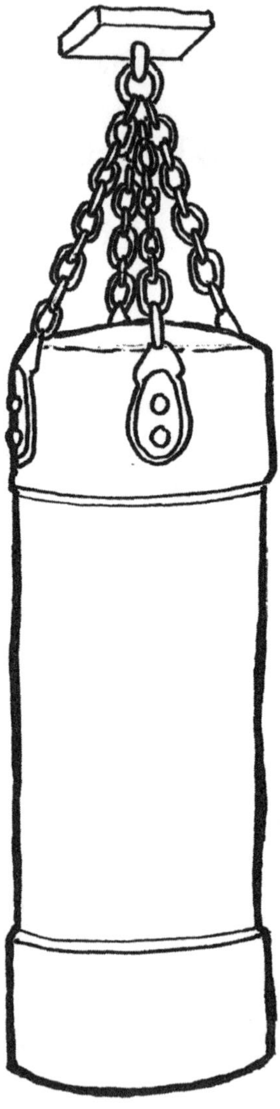

27 Learn to Throw a Punch.

I hope you never have to throw a punch. It's a memory that stays with you, and usually not a pleasant one. But there's a peppering of skunks on this earth, and someday, you may get forced into a showdown with one of them. I just want you to feel ready and confident in that moment, that you can handle yourself.

You'll know when it's about to happen, so get your head around the moment and confront your fear. Most of the power won't come from your arm; it'll come from your body. You have to lean into it; use your torso and your hips. Plant your feet, punch with your whole body, and then, right away, draw your hand back in case you have to defend yourself.

If the skunk persists after the haymaker you've thrown, then keep your feet under you, start to slowly circle your opponent (harder to hit a moving target), and square your fists to protect your face.

Again, I don't like the idea of violence, but hoping something bad doesn't happen shouldn't stop you from getting insurance. Learning how to throw a punch is insurance. Maybe we can find a heavy bag and practice.

28 Make Your Own Lunch for School.

You cannot fill a brown bag with gummy worms. You cannot pack 100 percent carbs or individual sacks of high-sodium snacks. You cannot liquid-lunch it with just chocolate milk. You cannot make sandwiches of straight marshmallow fluff. You cannot make choices solely on their "flingability." You cannot opt out and buy from the cafeteria. Nor can you go full hunger strike. Feed thyself, child.

But for five school days in a row, you can wake up fifteen minutes early and pack yourself a nutritious lunchtime meal. For one week, you can do that. If you need help with ideas or a trip to the grocery store, just let me know.

FOR LIAM

29 Buy or Make a Gift for Someone.

For some, the act of giving gifts comes naturally. For the rest of us, not so much. On birthdays, all we feel is panic. We tend to flail around on internet search engines with only the phrase "cool gifts" to guide our way.

It's not that we don't want to get the people we love something great; it's just . . . we struggle to come up with ideas. And then the gift giving feels like this heavy burden. Which is silly. It's supposed to be fun.

You're probably too young to feel the responsibility of gift giving, which is why I added this task to the list. Because taking the time to think about someone else, and then going out of your way to do something kind for them—that's a mark of maturity. That's called selflessness.

People love it when you think about them. They're happy for the gift, sure, but the fact that you thought about them is what they'll remember. So that's the accomplishment here: just considering another person for a while. What do they like to do? What do they talk about all the time? Let's say they're into reading—could you get them a book from the library? Or make them a bookmark?

For this task, you can choose to give someone a gift for their birthday or on a holiday, but trust me: There's nothing like an unexpected moment of "I was just thinking about you."

30 Volunteer Your Time for the Community.

This world functions through a blend of self-interest and grace. Let me explain.

The self-interest part keeps the peace: It's the stuff we do because we know there's something in it for us. For instance, we take out the trash to get an allowance. We bulldog our homework to get an A. We shoot endless hoops to win trophies. Self-interest is transactional, and because most everyone understands the formula, the peace is kept.

But the grace part *creates* the peace—acts of human goodwill that promise nothing in return. They remind us that we're all good, down deep. If you hold the door for someone, that's grace. If you help them carry something heavy, that's grace. And volunteering your time and talents to help other people—that's a huge, concentrated act of grace.

You may have your own ideas, but here are some approaches to volunteerism to get you started. And I'm ready to work alongside you, if you want company.

- Take a trash bag to a park, and pick up litter.
- Organize a neighborhood food drive for our local food bank.
- Donate your old toys to a hospital so sick kids can play with them.
- Bake cookies, and bring them to the local fire station.
- Help take care of a community garden for a day.

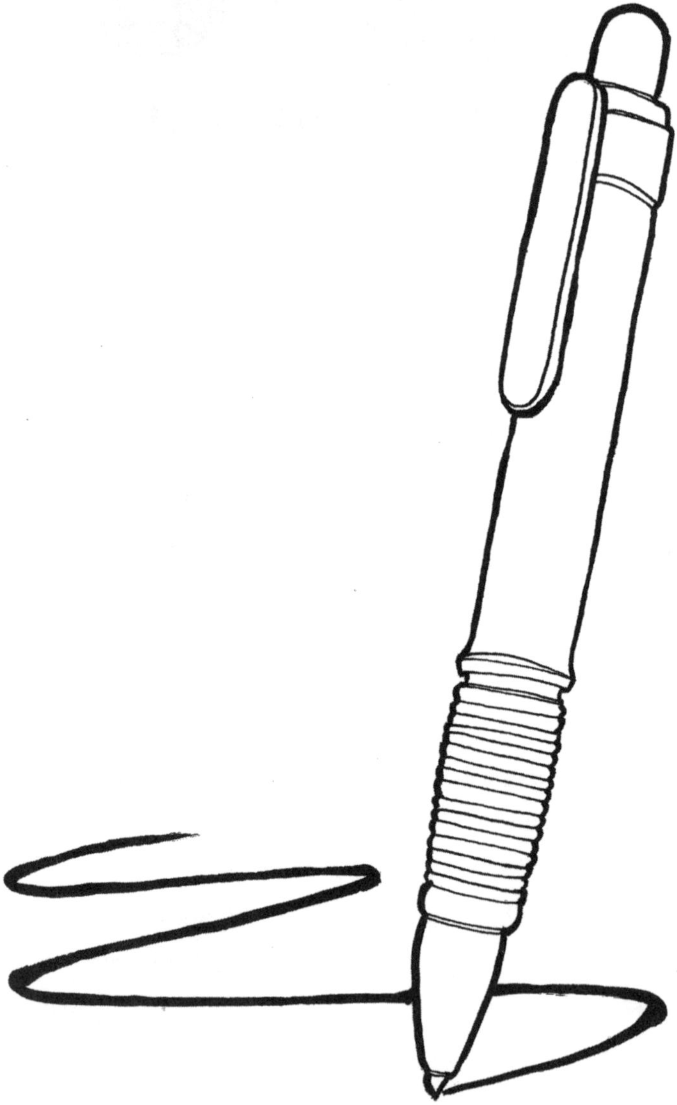

31 Write Me a Letter.

When you come across someone who knows how to write, it's like they're able to spark your brain with volts. They use words to suck you into their world; they get you to feel things. Even a well-written sticky note can lodge in your memory.

Sadly, good writing is a skill that's getting harder to come by. Maybe it's because of emojis? Maybe it's because of that always-on fire hose of episodes, games, memes, videos of dogs jumping into pools, aka the internet? With all that entertainment, who has time to read?

But I promise you, there will come a day when you write a note to your crush or an email to your boss's boss, and the way you write (if you're good at it) will stop them in their tracks. And they'll reread it. Because they like how your mind works.

So write me a letter. Plant yourself somewhere comfortable, get an actual pen and paper, and think. The silence will get to you at first. The blank page will render you speechless. But take it easy. Start with one idea. Let that one idea carry you to the next. And after a bit, you may find the pen humming.

Fill a full page, front and back. Here, I'll even give you the first line: "Hey there, most amazing parent in the universe . . ."

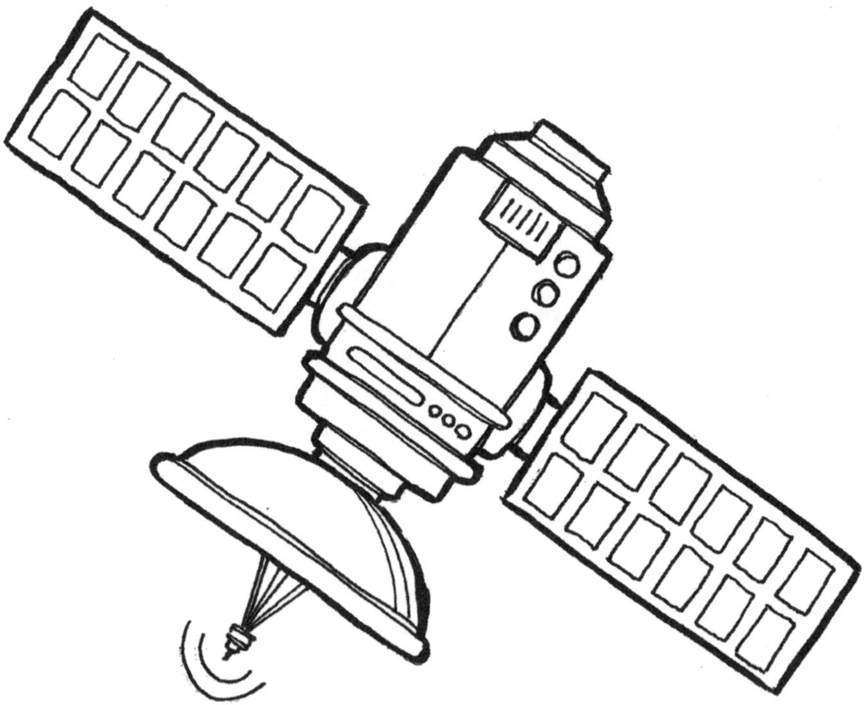

32

Explain to Me How the Phone Actually Works.

This one's easier than it sounds. It's cool if you find the answer on YouTube and then try to explain it to me in your own words or even if you just watch the video with me.

But there's a reason behind the ask: We take the miracles of the digital age for granted. We expect phones to work without caring enough to know how they work. For instance, I type a text and then—bloop—it shows up on someone's phone. But HOW?! Did the letters squish into microscopic dots and scoot through the air? Did that GIF of "Taylor Swift making a weird face" laser up to space and back? I want answers. And I think you're the one who can get them for me.

It's also good to bend your brain into unfamiliar shapes once in a while, to dig into subjects that are unfamiliar or even completely foreign. It can be a fun challenge. There are all sorts of interesting things to figure out—especially at your age—and if getting this phone is important to you, then we can do a little work toward understanding how it works.

So do some quick research, and break it down for me. We may not end up electrical engineers, but hey, we'll have a little more knowledge.

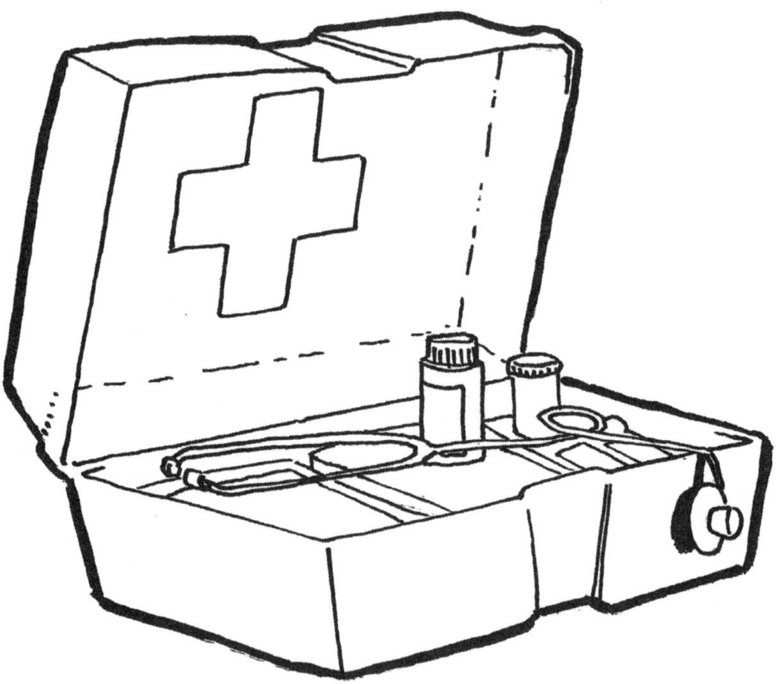

33 Get First Aid Certified.

A lot of people get weirded out by the human body, especially when the blood or the bones inside come out into the world. We recoil with an animal reflex—"Oh no, that shouldn't be there!"—which is perfectly normal.

But you and I both know that cuts, scrapes, bumps, and bruises happen. We have accidents sometimes; we wipe out. And in those situations, it's good to have a basic working knowledge of first aid. I don't need you to be a doctor or nurse. I just need you to build enough knowledge to overcome the "EWW!" instinct and help deal with whatever problem has come up. Because the more you know about a subject, the less freaky it is.

The Red Cross is an organization that offers classes you and I can take in one day. We could learn about how to treat burns or how to help someone who's choking. We could learn CPR, which is how you help someone who's having a breathing or heart emergency. And whatever we learn in that class may get you comfortable enough with the human body to maybe think about learning more. Who knows? Maybe it'll help you save someone down the line.

34 Walk Your Brother or Sister to School.

Let's pick a day when the weather's nice, when we've woken up with enough time to get a good breakfast into you and can leave the house without bananas urgency. Then, I'll stand at the door with my mug of coffee and send you out into the wild world.

You're old enough to navigate this neighborhood on your own. The walk isn't too far. The world will be waking up with you, people will be heading to work, squirrels will be chasing each other. You'll probably see other kids walking too.

The trick with this task is the responsibility for your brother or sister. They may want to hold your hand. They're going to need help safely crossing the streets. They may not know the route all that well, so they'll need your directions. Keep them on track. You can stop and smell some roses along the way, but don't get too distracted. Remember: You're on the clock.

Walking your sibling to school is kind of an analogy for a behavior you'll need your whole life: looking out for your family. Your friends are important, but they can drift in and out over the years. Your family is tied to you forever. If you can look out for them in the small moments, like walks to school, then you can look out for them with the big stuff. And they'll look out for you too.

[If you don't have any siblings, walking with a friend or neighbor will do.]*

MAGGIE

35 Care for an Animal.

This is hard for anyone younger than thirty to understand, but here goes: It's not all about you. Did you know that, in addition to you, there are currently eight billion people on this planet? And then a whole bunch of elephants, swordfish, beetles, trees, etc. Life is everywhere. And you're just a part of that story—an important part, but certainly not the whole story.

As a parent, I've learned that having someone depend on you is sacred: making sure they're fed, that they have a nice place to sleep, that they're learning things—making them feel cared for and safe. It's a big responsibility. It's a selfless responsibility. And I know you have the ability to take it on, even at your age.

So let's pick a life to care about. It could be a fish, a hermit crab, a hamster. It could be a worm you find outside. It could even be the family dog, as long as the responsibility for caring for its life is 100 percent yours for a bit; let's say a week. Your job is to watch over the animal, provide them with meals, and make sure that their poop is cleaned up, they're getting exercise, getting some love, and so on. I can't guarantee the animal will shower you with thanks, but honestly, that's a big part of this task: doing things for others with no expectation of a return.

36 Eat Vegetarian for One Week.

It's kind of interesting to challenge yourself to cut meat from your diet. No jerky. No hot dogs. No meatballs. No pepperoni. It's not easy, because, for a lot of us, meat is the main component of lunch or dinner. About 80 percent of the world is eating chicken, turkey, cow, pig, or fish on the regular. That's our go-to for protein.

But there's another way of eating entirely based on plants. And while that might sound boring to you, you'd be surprised at how interesting a vegetarian diet can be: smoothies, noodles, soups, veggie burgers, peanut butter, grain bowls, and crazy stuff like lentils and falafel. There are tons of options. Vegetarian food can be delicious.

Regardless of whether this feels insane or interesting, going vegetarian for a week will be a good stretch assignment for you. You're at an age when trying new things is met with resistance, but hey, overcoming resistance is part of the story here. You want a phone? Eat some beans.

I'm actually excited to help you out with this. We'll make some fun dinners.

NEW TIMES
EVERYDAY NEWS

37 Tell Me What's Going On in the World.

When you walk out the front door, it's easy to look straight ahead and think you've got it all figured out. But there are so many other people, each walking out their own front doors, each with their own soul. And they're all doing things! Driving to get a bagel, protesting court decisions on the street, attending rock festivals, making artificially intelligent robots . . . Whew, the list keeps going.

I don't expect you to have awareness of—much less care about—all that stuff. You're a kid; you're figuring out the basics. Why would the latest election cycle in Myanmar matter to you yet?

But a lot of the tasks in this book are about honoring the beginning of your consciousness. You're shaking off the easy haze of childhood. You're starting to notice your surroundings with new clarity. And for this task, I want you to lean into that feeling. Because the wider world will be yours someday, and if you make an effort to stay aware of it, you'll start connecting dots inside the human experience. Which creates compassion.

So find one big news story, learn about it on a couple different media platforms, and be prepared to have a conversation with me. Science news, political news, business or cultural news—it's your call. You tell me what's going on, I'll ask a few questions, and we'll talk about what it all might mean.

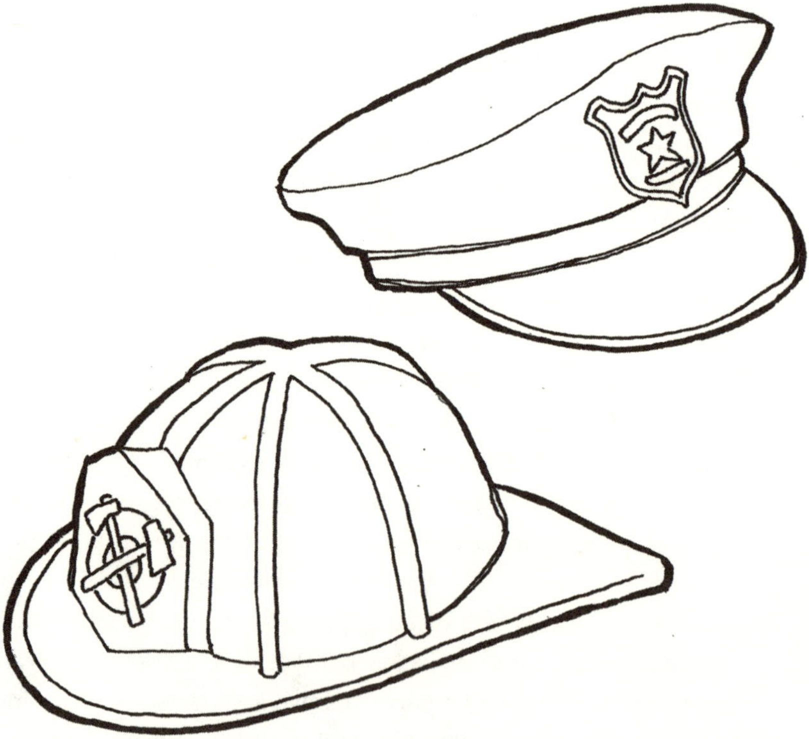

38 Tour the Local Police or Fire Station.

You probably don't think about cops or firefighters too much. We might see their cars and trucks whizz by once in a while, but if there's not an emergency, they kind of blend into the scenery of regular life.

It can be dangerous stuff, though. Imagine running into a burning house or stopping a crime in progress. Every day, cops and firefighters put their lives on the line to keep us safe.

So why do I want you to visit their headquarters? Because it's easy to see them as just a magical outcome of pressing 9-1-1 on our phones and not as real men and women doing hard, important jobs that benefit our lives quite a bit. By getting a tour of the places they work, you'll develop respect for the toughness of their professions.

At the police station, you'll learn about order. The laws we live by were set up to keep us all civil and friendly, and the police make sure we're not making bad decisions by breaking them.

At the fire station, you'll learn about rescue. Crazy accidents and catastrophes happen all the time, and while most people run to safety in those situations, firefighters run directly into the storm. When we're in trouble, they save us. You should see how that works.

I can set up these visits and go with you. Fire trucks and jail cells? It'll be cool.

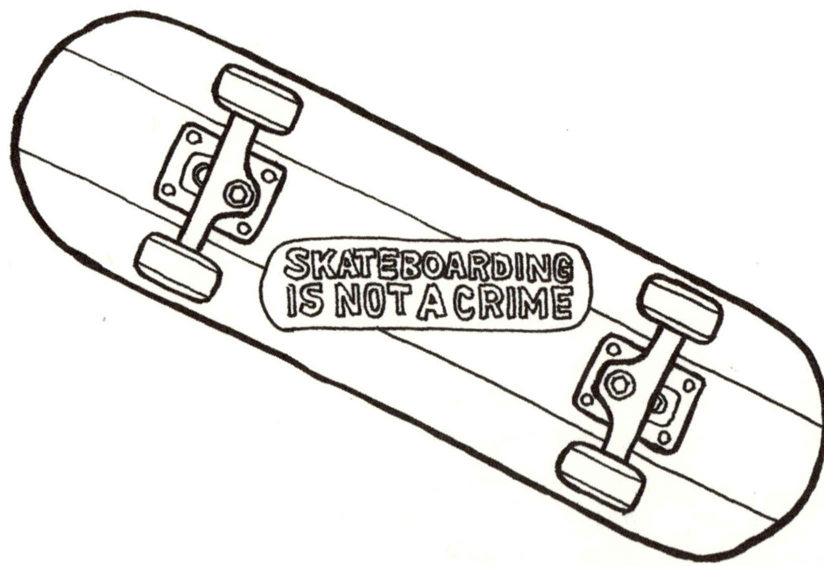
SKATEBOARDING
IS NOT A CRIME

39 Break a (Minor) Law.

Hold up. So far, your whole life has been rules—don't do that, do this. Nope, do this. And that's because I care about you. I've been trying to keep you safe. Before you knew the stove was hot or the knife was sharp or that cars make the street a dangerous place to wander, I had to tell you about it. I had to give you rules.

Well, I'm here to blow your mind: The rule-makers don't always get it right. For instance, people used to be allowed to smoke cigarettes in airplanes and restaurants—until they realized smoke was bad for everyone and changed the rule. And right now, they allow kids of all ages to have phones and unleashed access to the internet and social media, and maybe that's not the best idea either. 😬

The point is, as you grow up and assert your place in the world, it'll be important for you to not take everything you're told at face value. Question authority. Assess each situation, and rely on your own judgment to determine the right thing. You've got a good head on your shoulders and a moral heart; I trust you.

So for this task, I'm giving you the freedom to figure out a rule you think is stupid and then break it. I mean don't do anything reckless. Don't steal anything or hurt anyone—those are good rules (and besides, you'll end up in the slammer). But it could be a law your school put in place or (whoa!) a rule I put in place.

Just know this: There may be consequences. Most of our choices have consequences.

I'll be interested to see how this goes.

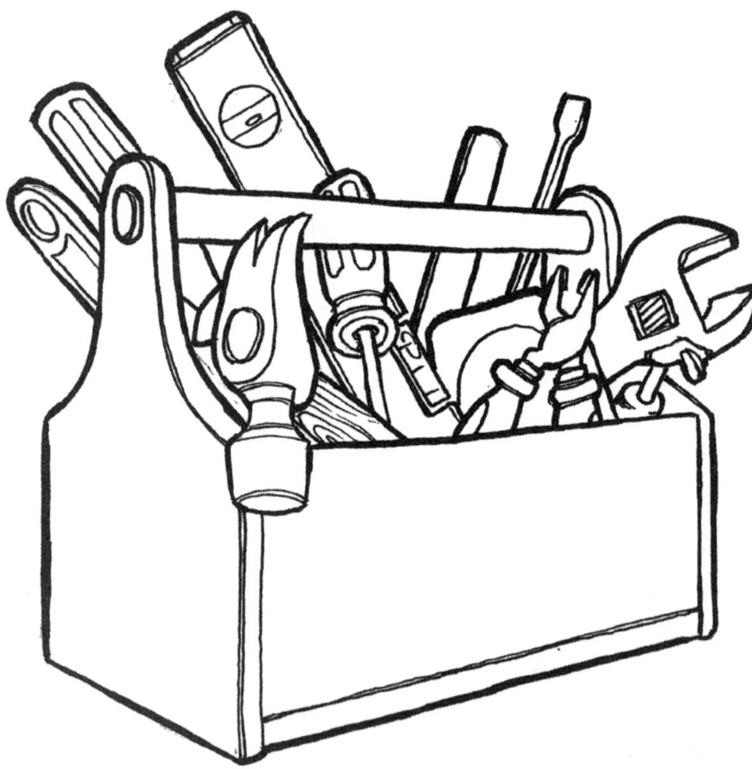

40 Build Something out of Wood with Me.

When we were kids in middle school, there was this class called Woodshop. For a semester, we were taught how to work with rulers, table saws, glue, nails, sanders, and lacquer. And at the end of the year, we had to turn in a big project. Some kids made step stools; some made bookshelves; some even made working lamps, with electrical cords that plugged in and everything.

There was this high level of craftsmanship and care at each stage: getting the measurements just right. Running raw pine through the buzz saw. Clamping the seams nice and tight while the glue dried. Painting the finished product. And at the end, we arrived at something that looked surprisingly impressive, like something that would've blended in just fine on a shelf in a home goods store.

Learning to work with wood is a skill you'll come back to throughout your life. Houses and furniture are made of wood, right? Well, sometimes, houses and furniture need repairing. It's good to be able to step up and do things yourself once in a while.

Woodworking has some danger to it—sharp saws, heavy hammers, chemical varnish—and that's kind of what I want to introduce with this project. Let's find something simple to build together, like a birdhouse or a pencil box or a bookshelf. We'll locate well-organized instructions online, head to the hardware store, assemble our materials, and put our heads together. It'll be fun and tricky and new, all at the same time.

41 Read a Book.

Look: I picked out three good ones. Which seems the most exciting?

- *The Adventures of Huckleberry Finn*: A young boy runs away from his no-good father, finds a raft, and floats down the Mississippi River, which creates all kinds of adventures, helping him grow up.
- *Siddhartha*: A young man leaves a comfortable home and heads into the wilds of ancient India, searching for the meaning of life.
- *To Kill a Mockingbird*: The story of a lawyer told through the eyes of his daughter as he fights for the life of a Black man unjustly accused of a crime during a very racist period in the United States.

Why these books? Because they're equal parts fun ride and wisdom. Because they'll push you to think. They'll teach you about morality and the human condition, and they will shake how you see the world. Parts of them are a little grown-up, but I can talk you through anything that feels weird.

In the age of screens, reading probably seems like a throwback pastime, but it's really good for developing your brain because it requires more effort from your imagination. As you go through this life, I hope there's always a novel next to your bed. It's been a friend to me since I was a kid—the quiet work of reading, the peace and quiet of it while your mind fills with story. It's magic.

Hey, bonus points if you read all three. Ice cream on me.

NW
NE
SW
SE

42

Pick a Location at Least Two Miles from Home. Navigate Us There Without GPS.

If you haven't caught on yet, the whole point of this book is to teach you self-reliance. Because sometimes phones lose power. The Wi-Fi goes out. The satellites quit communicating. At times like those, you've got nothing to rely on but your own wits. So, for this task, let's make sure those wits are razor-sharp.

I'm betting you know our neighborhood pretty well. You've driven these streets with me: to school, to Target, to the movie theater. Let's test your skills and see if you have a directional sense of the place we live.

Pick a location at least two miles from our home, and act as our navigator: Tell me when to turn right or left or go straight, and we'll follow your instructions. If we get lost, no worries; I'll get us back on track—until eventually, we arrive.

We can drive or even walk if you're up for it. Give me a reason to kill an afternoon with you; I'll take it every time.

THE ROAD NOT TAKEN
HOPE IS THE THING WITH FEATHERS
STILL I RISE

Memorize a Poem. 43

The idea of poetry feels pretty soft these days. But for thousands of years, it was a big-deal art form. Poets used rhymes and rhythm to tell stories and paint pictures in people's heads and entertain them.

I guess popular music replaced poetry. But for this task, you can't memorize a song. We don't want the ghost of the melody playing along in your head, distracting you from the words. We just want to feel the words.

Pick a poem by one of the greats: Rumi, Dickinson, Yeats, Neruda, Millay, Silverstein. Find one that connects with you. I'm happy to help you dig around in the library or on the internet. Also, it's got to be at least fourteen lines.

Read it once through. Then, read just the first line; really drink it up. Try to say it with your eyes closed. Then onto the next line, and the next, until you know the poem backward and forward. When you're ready, recite it to me from memory.

It's good to carry a poem around with you, tucked away in your head. It becomes a secret piece of you, a truth that you carry around. That's why I want you to find one that really connects. And then, someday, you'll bust it out at a dinner and blow people away. The room will get as quiet as a church. They'll hang on your every word.

R.I.P.
GRANNY ANNIE
BELOVED
AUGUST 21, 1923-
FEBRUARY 26, 2018

44 Visit a Cemetery.

Oh, death.

For lots of people, death is an uncomfortable topic. Because if not this life, then . . . what? Where do our spirits go? It's the great unknown, the great mystery. And not knowing can make people a little nauseous.

But thinking about the end of your story can help you appreciate the electricity of all the other parts—the parts you're living right now. If we're lucky, we'll both get a good long century on this planet, and there's so much to experience while we're here. Skateboarding. Bounce castles. Brazil. Pizza. Man, oh man. Pizza.

One gentle way of getting comfortable with the idea of death is walking through a cemetery. You'll feel the sun on the back of your neck. You'll hear the breeze brushing the leaves. You'll sit with that quiet, reading the dates on headstones, and you'll think about all the souls who have traveled this earth, all with their own hopes, feelings, love stories. You'll start to realize that we're all connected, that love is the antidote to fear, that time doesn't really exist, and then . . .

Well, you'll figure it out. You'll have your own thoughts. But let's just go, you and me, and walk quietly and think about our lives. How lucky we are to have each other.

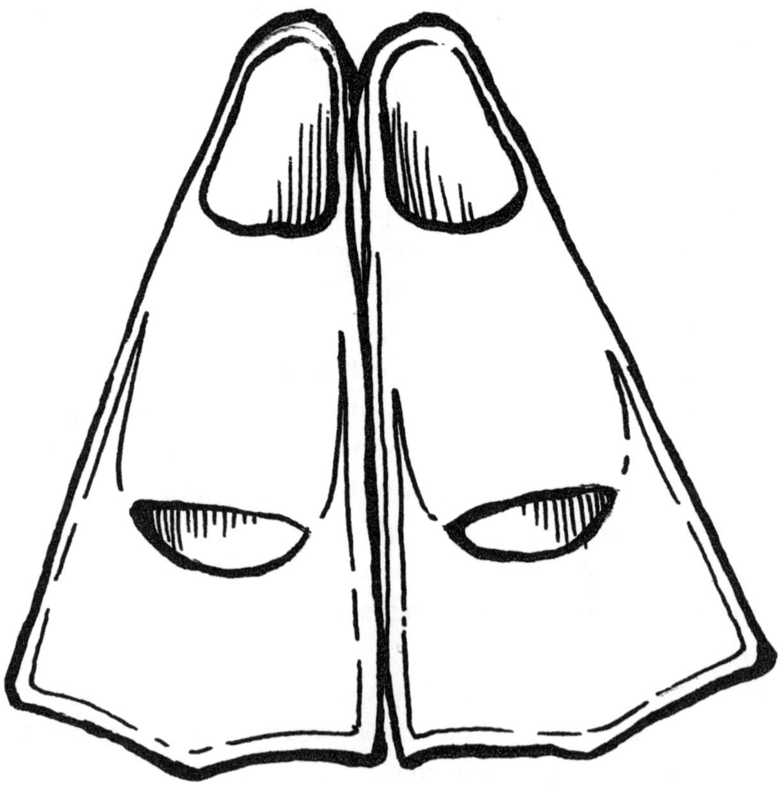

45 Swim One Hundred Meters.

We don't have gills. I wish we had gills. Then, we could walk under the water and never have to learn how to swim. But gills for humans are probably a thousand years out on the evolutionary timeline.

Did you ever see anyone who really knows how to swim, who can cut through the water like a fish? Like they were born for it? It's kind of beautiful to see. And I think we can get you there too.

"Why do I have to do this?" you ask. Because this planet is, like, 75 percent water. Pools, lakes, oceans. There are going to be times when you'll be hanging out with friends, and water will be the main source of fun. Crashing into the waves, playing Marco Polo. You'll want to be part of it. There may even be times when you have to get somewhere, and your only option is to swim. It's one of those clutch life skills.

Why one hundred meters? That's about the length of a football field, which is long enough to test your endurance—your muscles and lungs. It'll give you the skills to cross any pool and the confidence to approach most bodies of water without fear. While we're at it, I should probably show you how to float and tread water.

I can teach you the basics. Or I can get you lessons. But this is worthwhile and important and totally the best alternative to growing gills.

Build a Fire. 46

You've heard your whole life not to play with fire, that it's dangerous. And it is. But there comes a time when you have to approach danger in order to master it. And I think you're ready to learn how to deal with hot flames.

It helps if you treat fire as a tool to be respected versus something to be played with. Knives are dangerous, right? But we need them to cut food. Cars and bikes can be dangerous too, but they help us get around. That's why we take the time to learn to use things properly: so that we can access their value while minimizing the danger.

Building a fire isn't too complicated. We'll need a clear space, with nothing flammable nearby. The fireplace is a good, safe option. So is a firepit outside, which you can construct with rocks. You'll gather small twigs and leaves, which will get the fire started, and larger branches, which will keep it fueled. Everything will need to be dry. Then, I'll show you how to build a small tower with them so that the fire lights and stays lit.

Honestly? You might get a tiny burn on your finger. But small burns aren't a huge deal; we'll patch you up. And the burn is how we learn the fire's rules.

PS: This is a task you have to do with my supervision. Non-negotiable, kiddo.

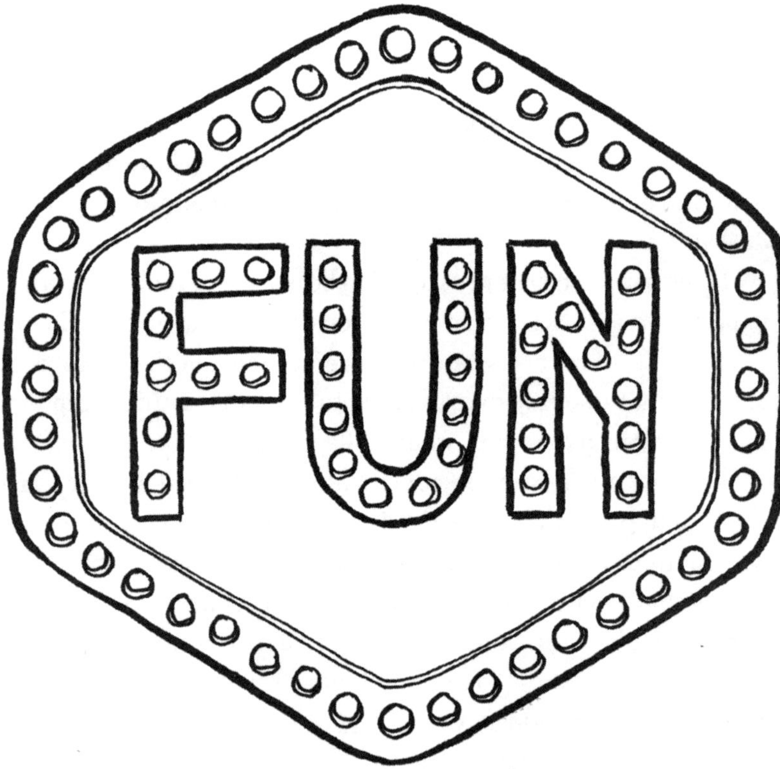
FUN

47 Let Me Take You and Your Friends Somewhere to Hang Out.

Cringe, my dad is laaame. OMG, why is he forcing this uncomfortable situation? He's so suss skibidi whatever.

C'mon, now, it doesn't have to be all that dramatic. It could be simple. We could take your friends to the movies. Or go eat at a diner. Or go to a trampoline gym or water park. I don't need to shoot the waterslides alongside you necessarily, although I do love a good waterslide. We could go to the park and play soccer. (I promise not to dominate.) You could invite me into one of your gaming sessions.

I'm just kind of curious to see what you're like with your friends, to see the person you're becoming inside that comfort. And then, I'll leave you guys alone and go back to doing my thing.

So use your imagination. Pick something FUN to do. I'll talk to the other parents, and we'll make it happen.

SAFE

48

Save Enough Money to Buy the Phone Yourself.

Step one: Locate the phone you want.

Step two: Figure out how much it costs.

Step three: Do some chores! Hoard that birthday cash! Hold a yard sale! Become a ghostbuster! Just find a way to earn some money.

You're at an age when many of your needs and desires are paid for: food, shelter, clothing, toys, bicycles—all of it, covered. Well, I'm here to tell you: That gravy train doesn't run forever. The tracks stop when you become an adult, self-reliant, on your own. And between now and then, there are some nonessential items you're going to want that will require you to do a little work. This phone is one of them.

The phone, *nonessential*?! Yes, it is. It's a modern-day luxury. So if you want one, let's get to work and earn it. (You can also try to sweet-talk one of your relatives into giving you their old phone. I'll allow it.)

And don't worry—once the phone is purchased, I'll cover the monthly service charges for you.

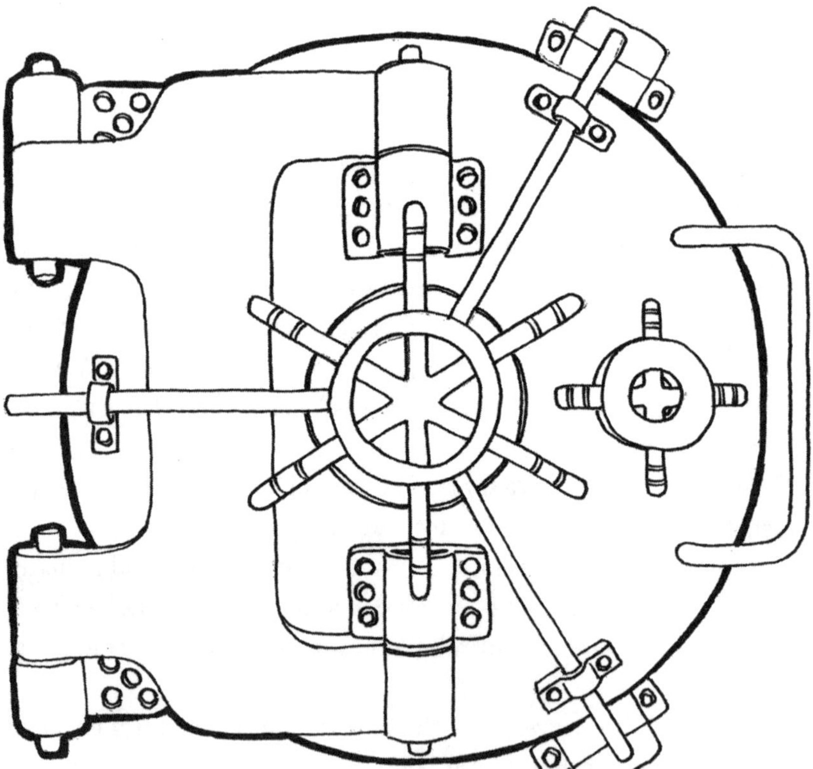

49 Manage That Money in a Bank.

Money used to be almost 100 percent paper bills and metal coins, but lately, it's become more and more digital, meaning it only exists as numbers on the internet.

Managing money through banking apps is something you'll want to get accustomed to because you'll be using them your whole life. And you should get started on it early, while I'm nearby and can help. One of the mistakes we make as parents is not showing kids how to be responsible with money when they're still young. You'll want to learn and make mistakes with me while the consequences are small and controllable.

Here are the steps we'll need to take:

1. Pick out a bank. I like banks that have a good reputation for security, have been around awhile, and have branches nearby so that I can talk to someone if I need help.
2. We'll open a savings account for you and download the app. The app will live on my phone, and I can show you your money whenever you want.
3. Pick out a password that only you can remember. Make it a tricky one because your money's on the other side of it.
4. We'll deposit your money into the bank, where it will grow. (The bank pays you for letting them hold it.)
5. Then, it's yours to manage. You can add more when you get it or take some out and spend it, but remember: Your goal for this task is to save.

50

Turn Fourteen.

Hahahahaha. Dad joke.

Ideally, it would be great if you could turn fourteen before this device gets into your hands—but they say age is just a number. Everyone's different; we develop at different speeds. If I get the feeling that your maturity exceeds your biological age and I think you're ready for a phone before turning fourteen, maybe I can make a concession. Maybe . . .

Checklist

1. Do the laundry. ☐
2. Play a game of chess. ☐
3. Get paid for a skill. ☐
4. Sit in a room. For fifteen minutes. Without doing anything. ☐
5. Write a thank-you note. Make it count. ☐
6. Do the grocery shopping. ☐
7. Cook a full dinner. Serve it to the family. Clean up. ☐
8. Babysit for a night. ☐
9. Make me a playlist. ☐
10. Bike to a friend's house and back, at least a half mile away. ☐
11. Spend some time with old folks. ☐
12. Play me one-on-one in basketball. A full game, to twenty-one. ☐
13. Go for a long walk in the wild. ☐
14. Grow a vegetable from seed. ☐
15. Catch a fish. ☐
16. Approach someone you don't know well. ☐
17. Come to work with me for a day. ☐
18. Play me a song on an instrument. ☐
19. Record your thoughts in a journal for a month. ☐
20. Write down five questions you've always wanted answers to. I'll do my best to answer them. ☐
21. Attend a religious service or two. ☐
22. Write down your top ten beliefs. ☐
23. Run a 5k. ☐
24. Go on a weekend road trip with me. ☐

25. Clean the bathroom. ☐
26. Spend a night in the woods camping. ☐
27. Learn to throw a punch. ☐
28. Make your own lunch for school. ☐
29. Buy or make a gift for someone. ☐
30. Volunteer your time for the community. ☐
31. Write me a letter. ☐
32. Explain to me how the phone actually works. ☐
33. Get first aid certified. ☐
34. Walk your brother or sister to school. ☐
35. Care for an animal. ☐
36. Eat vegetarian for one week. ☐
37. Tell me what's going on in the world. ☐
38. Tour the local police or fire station. ☐
39. Break a (minor) law. ☐
40. Build something out of wood with me. ☐
41. Read a book. ☐
42. Pick a location at least two miles from home. Navigate us there without GPS. ☐
43. Memorize a poem. ☐
44. Visit a cemetery. ☐
45. Swim one hundred meters. ☐
46. Build a fire. ☐
47. Let me take you and your friends somewhere to hang out. ☐
48. Save enough money to buy the phone yourself. ☐
49. Manage that money in a bank. ☐
50. Turn fourteen. ☐

About the Author

ADAM FERGUSON was born in New York City but raised in the suburbs of North Jersey. His parents were saddled with the baggage of hardscrabble childhoods but worked tirelessly to give him and his siblings something better. His brother is a soulful artist, and his sister is an executive baller, but he doesn't call enough to tell them how proud he is. The first shock to his system came from reading books, but it never really translated to a love of school. He grew his hair out as teenager, dug the rebellion of it, but never lied to himself about the system or the game. He plays guitar every day but accepts he'll never access Jimmy Page's god-given feel for the damn thing. He likes to snowboard, but his cool buckles at high speeds. He's usually wearing a baseball cap but only because the brim narrows his focus. He roots for the underdog, as a rule, but makes an exception for the New York Yankees. He's all contentment living in the Midwest, but when someone yells, "O-H," he feels inauthentic replying. He keeps his chin up and his shoulders back but spills tears at small unnoticed acts of humanity. He's good to see the world once in a while but happiest within the quiet domesticity of home.

Most importantly, though, he's still captivated and spellbound by the girl he fell for at age nineteen and so grateful for the three kids they made together, whose talents and perspectives continually knock him sideways. No buts about it.